GOD'S
Chocolate Chips
Daily Doses of Heaven's Chocolate to Sweeten Your Life

Erin Wilmer

WESTBOW
PRESS*
A DIVISION OF THOMAS NELSON
& ZONDERVAN

WestBow Press books may be ordered through booksellers or by contacting:

WestBow Press
A Division of Thomas Nelson & Zondervan
1663 Liberty Drive
Bloomington, IN 47403
www.westbowpress.com
1 (866) 928-1240

ISBN: 978-1-9736-8328-5 (sc)
ISBN: 978-1-9736-8330-8 (hc)
ISBN: 978-1-9736-8329-2 (e)

Library of Congress Control Number: 2020900338

Print information available on the last page.

WestBow Press rev. date: 01/28/2020

Dedication

I DEDICATE THIS BOOK TO God. Thank you for loving me in spite of myself and for choosing me as a vessel.

It goes without saying that my husband, Steve Wilmer, is no doubt my biggest fan, and he is always poking, prodding, pushing, pulling, and challenging me to be all that God has created me to be.

My children—Judah, Josiah, Joi, and Jayna. The greatest gift God ever gave me was mothering the four of you. Remember to stay on the winning team!

To the women of my life who mentor me, love me, and guide me—my mother, Lillian; my grandmother, Frances; my sisters, Jill and Felicia, my spiritual mothers, Cheryl and Kelly, and my spiritual sister, Milana, who I call my voices of reason-my life is richer because of all of you.

Acknowledgements

SPECIAL THANKS TO MY SISTERS in the faith, Kari Dunham & Karen Merritt-Wade for using your time and giftings to bring this book to life.

Introduction

I INVITE YOU TO TAKE this thirty-one-day journey with me. Each day we encounter God's presence in everyday occurrences. He reveals himself in everything we encounter, experience, and endure. He is somewhere, behind the scenes, working on our behalf. And if we look closely enough, if we shut out all the noise of the day, we will see and hear him. God is the essence of chocolate; everything is sweeter with him in it!

$\mathcal{D}ay\ 1$

CLOGGED PORES

DURING A RECENT FACIAL, THE therapist began lecturing me on clogged pores. She explained how the pores can get clogged with too much secretion of sebum, with dry and dead skin cells, or with normal everyday dirt and filth. She explained that if I didn't keep my face clean by using a regular skin-care regimen, it could cause discoloration, and my skin would be unable to display its natural beauty. As I listened to her, I wondered what areas of my life were clogged. Where have I allowed dry and dead things to stay in my life? Where did I need to wash off the everyday dirt and filth of the world? Did I need a spiritual facial? Hmmmm, do you? I go every month to have my skin cleaned and my pores unclogged. How much more often should I go and lay on the table of my Creator and allow him to unclog my life's pores? More than once a month, that's for sure! Each day we can take all our cares, concerns, and worries to our Father. He will exfoliate us so our true beauty will shine. Be blessed, my friends, and get those pores unclogged.

Daily Prayer

God, today help me to allow you to make me over. Let me never be ashamed to lay before you for a spiritual cleansing. My desire is that I am a reflection of you. In Jesus's name, Amen.

Scripture Reference

Wash me clean of my iniquity and cleanse me from my sin. (Psalm 51:2 English Standard Bible)

Self-Reflection

In what ways do you need your life pores unclogged?

_____

_____

_____

_____

_____

_____

_____

_____

_____

_____

_____

_____

_____

$\mathcal{D}ay\ 2$

3D GLASSES

I REMEMBER THE FIRST TIME I experienced a movie in 3D. It was so realistic! The colors were so vibrant. The sound, crystal clear, and the action scenes were amazing. I felt like I was right there on the screen with the actors. I felt myself feeling every punch and dodging every bullet. Everything was so exaggerated. The punches were so realistic that when they punched someone on the screen, my head bounced back as if I were getting punch. Now this was the way to watch a movie!

Then they created the 3D rides. Talk about an adventure! Imagine with me entering a small room with nothing on the walls. You buckle up, and the lights go out. Suddenly, you are in the middle of a river, coming up on a waterfall. You go over. You see yourself falling and falling, and then you feel the hard hit as you land. There is a brick wall; you crash into it, and your boat is destroyed. You feel water as you hang onto a log that washes you ashore. Suddenly, you are surrounded by cannibals. Arrows of fire come at you. You hear them hitting on your left and on your right. There is no escape. Then, the hero of the film suddenly appears and rescues you by helicopter. And the ride is over. The lights come on, and you are in the same small room you were in before the ride started. Wow! You realize none of it was real. It was all an illusion from the 3D experience.

Have you ever gone through something in your life that was 3D? The circumstances were so exaggerated, so realistic, that you believed everything the situation was telling you? You just got laid off from your job and will never find another one like it. Your child is strung out on drugs and is never coming out of it. You have diabetes, and it is incurable. You had a heart attack, and the next one will kill you. You have cancer and three months to live. I don't know what 3D ride you are on right now, but I can tell you the hero of the movie is on his way! Just over that cliff, just over that waterfall, right after that tenth arrow of fire, he will show up and rescue you. God is a way-maker, a miracle worker, a promise keeper, and the light in the darkness. And he has 3D glasses! He will find you no matter where you are. Hold on—the hero is on his way!

Daily Prayer

God, remind me that you are my hero. You win every fight. You wrote the ending to each chapter of my life, and you don't want to spoil it for me, but ... I win! Help me to remember you are my refuge and my strength, and you will help me when I am in trouble. In Jesus's name, Amen.

Scripture Reference

God is a safe place to hide, ready to help when we need him. (Psalm 46:1 The Message Bible)

Self-Reflection

What fights do you need God to win right now?

_____

_____

_____

_____

_____

_____

_____

_____

_____

_____

_____

_____

_____

$\mathcal{D}ay$ 3

THAT BABY!

WHEN OUR OLDEST DAUGHTER, JOI, was a baby, she was absolutely adorable. Her laughter could light up a room. Her smile could melt the hardest of hearts. There is a three-year difference between our youngest son and oldest daughter. As a matter of fact, before she came along, he was the baby; all attention was centered on him. When he learned that she was coming, both he and his brother were so excited. We would talk and sing to her in the womb. But the day she arrived, things changed. He saw she was getting all of the attention. and his excitement quickly went to boredom. "Mom, that baby is crying!" "Mom, that baby needs its diaper changed!" "Mom, that baby is hungry!"

When she was about six months old, he learned she could laugh, and the one thing she thought was hilarious was him! He would sit with her for hours, making her laugh. He would pretend to hit himself. He would make goofy faces. He would even get on all four and bark just like a dog. And she loved every minute of it. She would just laugh and laugh at her big brother. The more she laughed, the more comical he became. Pretty soon, those two were inseparable. To this day, they are close and entertain each other constantly.

I began to ponder joy and laughter. They both have the ability to change any situation, lighten any room, heal any hurt, even change the world. When is the last time you had a good hearty laugh? So much so your side hurt and your temples throbbed? Tears rolled down your cheeks. You even almost peed your pants.

Too long? Well, my friends, it's time! Time to LOL! LMBO! ROTFL! Laugh out loud! Laughing my butt off! Roll on the floor laughing! Find that one movie that cracks you up. Or the one TV series you love to watch that never fails to make you laugh. Go ahead, give it a try. I dare you. You will feel so much better. I promise!

Daily Prayer

God, today remind me to enjoy the journey of my life. Help me to not be so uptight over things I have no control over. Help me to smile from within, so it can exude outside me. In Jesus's name, Amen.

Scripture Reference

These things I have spoken to you, that my joy may be in you, and that your joy may be full. (John 15:11 New King James Version)

Extra Thought

Happiness is fickle and requires happy circumstances. Joy, on other hand, sticks around. It doesn't get chased off by trouble.

Self-Reflection

What are you joyful about?

_____

_____

_____

_____

_____

_____

_____

_____

_____

_____

_____

_____

_____

_____

$\mathscr{D}ay$ 4

COMBAT BOOTS

 AS A MILITARY VETERAN OF twenty-four years, the one thing I never worried about was what to wear to work. Every day for twenty-four years, I wore the same shirt, the same pants, the same boots, and the same hairstyle. There was no debate about what to wear. I got up, I got dressed, and I reported for duty. Since retiring, I have started a new career, one that requires me to look a certain way: professional, smart, successful, and accomplished. I have to dress in a way that attracts the right people: professional, smart, successful, accomplished, and wealthy. Dress to impress. No big deal, right? Wrong! For a military girl who grew up a tomboy, this is a very big deal. I spend a large part of my morning, toiling over what to wear, wishing I could just put on my uniform and combat boots because that is what I was used to. I am comfortable in my uniform, and I know who I am. In these civilian clothes, I feel awkward, unsure, and unstable, especially in these heels. Who wears these? I can't tell you how many times I have stumbled and even fallen in heels. I wonder why God would put me in a career so far from what I am used to, so foreign and so uncomfortable.

Have new challenges come up in your life that have you out of your comfort zone? Are you being drawn to the unfamiliar, the unknown, and you know without a shadow of doubt it is God who is drawing you there? Is it time to give up your combat boots for some heels? Well, my friend, climb in the car, get on the passenger side, and buckle your seat belt for the ride. Outside your comfort zone is where the magic happens. Throw out those old combat boots, close that chapter of your life, and walk into the new chapter God has for you. I promise you will not be disappointed. And you won't even miss those boots.

Daily Prayer

God, today help me to not be afraid to launch out into the deep. Help me to throw away my comfortable, old combat boots and my "comfort zone" banner, and let me follow your will and destiny for my life. In Jesus's name, Amen.

Scripture Reference

He said, "Throw the net off the right side of the boat and see what happens." They did what he said. All of a sudden there were so many fish in it, they weren't strong enough to pull it in. (John 21:6 The Message Bible)

Self-Reflection

In what ways are you staying in your comfort zone?

_____

_____

_____

_____

_____

_____

_____

_____

_____

_____

_____

_____

_____

$\mathcal{D}$ay 5

EGGS AND SAUSAGE

EARLY IN MY MARRIAGE, I secretly planned to surprise my husband with breakfast in bed. I was so excited! I got up extra early to prepare a feast fit for a king of bacon, sausage, eggs, grits, and biscuits. As I hummed to myself, I imagined the look on his face. He would be so surprised, so pleased, so touched! I knew I was going to score some major points with him.

After I finished cooking this special feast, I carefully laid each item on his plate. The serving sizes were perfect, just the right amount so he could fully enjoy his breakfast. It was beautiful. I finished my masterpiece with a tall glass of orange juice and headed up the stairs to wake him. I entered the room, placed the tray in front of him, and gently shook him. "Wake up, baby," I said. "Look what I have for you." He arose with the strangest look on his face. It was almost as if he had seen a ghost. He was not surprised. He just sat there for a minute. The enthusiasm and excitement quickly left my body. My thoughts began to race. *What? What did I do? What's wrong? What? You don't like it?* He grabbed me and hugged me. Now I was really confused. *What in the world is going on?* I wondered.

"Erin," he said, "I dreamed this! I dreamed you were going to bring me breakfast in bed. And when you woke me up in the dream, I yelled and screamed at you for waking me up. I was mean and cruel to you, and you began crying. I saw this in my dream, before it happened." His face showed utter disbelief.

As he sat there trying to make sense of it all, my mind quickly went to my Father in heaven. He loves me so much! He saw how excited I was to do this special thing for my husband, so he visited him in his dream to make sure he did not crush my feelings. I felt so loved at that very moment, tears formed in my eyes. It reminded me how God is always there, no matter what life may bring my way. He is there, along with my big brother, Jesus, interceding for me, protecting me, shielding me from things I can't see. We are not in this world alone; we have advocates who will never leave their posts. They have our backs.

Daily Prayer

God, today remind me that you are always there, behind the scenes, interceding for me. Remind me I am never alone, that you will never leave me or break up with me. In Jesus's name, Amen.

Scripture Reference

Be strong. Take courage. Don't be intimidated. Don't give them a second thought because God, your God, is striding ahead of you. He's right there with you. He won't let you down; he won't leave you. (Deuteronomy 31:6 The Message Bible)

Self-Reflection

In what ways has God intervened for you?

_____

_____

_____

_____

_____

_____

_____

_____

_____

_____

_____

_____

_____

_____

Day 6

Monkey See, Monkey Do

Our children are our pride and joy. They are little replicas of us. They say what we say, do what we do, act like we act. They end up resembling us so much that at times, it can be embarrassing. Have you ever been out with friends when your two-year-old yells a four-letter word after dropping his fork on the floor? You politely smile because you know exactly where he learned that word. How about when your five-year-old repeats something you said about your cousin behind his or her back? "My mommy says you don't know when to go home. You are always overstaying your welcome."

When our children display traits we don't like about ourselves, we want to punish or discipline them. Traits like lying, cheating, lusts of the flesh, and stealing, traits we don't want anyone to know we still struggle with. No one knows you cheat on your taxes by fudging a number here or there. No one knows about that extra five minutes you put on your time card every now and then. No one knows you really didn't work eight hours at work yesterday because you were strolling through Facebook, Twitter, Instagram, or Snap Chat. No one knows you are secretly contemplating having an affair. Or maybe you already did. Do you take a pen or two from work because they have way too many? When you are in Walmart, do you "test" the grapes to see if it is a good bunch? I began to think about the saying, "Monkey see, monkey do." Why do so many children repeat their parents' behaviors? How many people do you know have alcoholic fathers who end up becoming alcoholics? How many people with divorced parents end up in a

20

divorce? Understand that we all have choices, but the behaviors we witnessed all our lives often become our normal. You can break this cycle if you come in contact with the One who makes all things new. He has the ability to break any bad habits in your life, no matter what they are. Of course, it will take your cooperation—unless you like being the monkey.

Daily Prayer

God, today help me to be mindful that whether I want it to be or not, my life is a testimony, and it speaks loudly to others. Help me to always remember to represent you in all I say and do. In Jesus's name, Amen.

Scripture Reference

Here's another way to put it: You're here to be light, bringing out the God-colors in the world. God is not a secret to be kept. We're going public with this, as public as a city on a hill. If I make you light-bearers, you don't think I'm going to hide you under a bucket, do you? I'm putting you on a light stand. Now that I've put you there on a hilltop, on a light stand-shine! Keep open house; be generous with your lives. By opening up to others, you'll prompt people to open up with God, this generous Father in heaven. (Matthew 5:16 The Message Bible).

Self-Reflection

How is your light shining?

_____

_____

_____

_____

_____

_____

_____

_____

_____

_____

_____

_____

_____

_____

Day 7

MY BEST FRIEND

WE MET WHEN I WAS eighteen. It was the later part of 1988. It was a crowded room, full of smoke. I was feeling shy, and she was fun and vibrant. She was everything I wanted to be—the life of the party, fearless, larger than life. So we became friends. We spent so much time together. We were together when I was happy and when I was sad. When she was around, I was bold and sometimes careless. Other times, she just sat there in silence as I waddled in self-pity. She sat with me through my worst days. She was with me when I made some of my worst decisions.

As the years passed, I began to notice she was never there on my good days. She was never around when I made the right choices or the right decisions. After more than twenty-five years, I began to question her loyalty. I could no longer tell if she was for me or against me. On the surface, she was still fun, fearless, and the life of the party. But on the inside, she was depressing, sad, and almost suicidal. I started not to want her around as much. When she called, I ignored her calls, her urges, and her begging. Finally, I decided I wanted to break up with her. I realized she never added anything good to my life. I had been deceived this entire time. She didn't care about me. She wasn't for me. As a matter of fact, she was slowly killing me. With each encounter, I was slowly dying. She wanted me to stay sad, depressed, and dependent on her.

I began to pray and ask God to help me break up with her. I knew I couldn't do it on my own; I was going to need divine intervention.

I prayed and prayed and prayed. Finally, one hot summer day, I told her, "It's over. I no longer desire you. I no longer need you. You can no longer be a part of my life." She just sat there. She didn't believe me. What I didn't tell you earlier is I'd tried to break up with her several times before. I always came back. Therefore, she just didn't believe me. I knew she was thinking, *You'll be back. You always come back.* What she didn't realize was that this time, my mind was made up. Not only had I been praying for God to help me break up with her, but I prayed that he would change my mind about her. I was praying he would remove every taste of her from my very essence. And you know what? He did! At age forty-six, I had my last drink of alcohol. She is completely gone from my life! Oh, she tries to come back, but each time I see her now, I see her for what she truly is, a curse, an addiction. She is not my friend.

Do you suffer with an addiction? It could be recreational drugs, illegal drugs, nicotine, caffeine, sex, food, or any other drug of choice. You may say, "I am not an alcoholic," or, "I only get high once in a while. I have it completely under control." Ask yourself, "Why do I drink? Why do I get high? What is the emotion tied to when I drink? Is it after a long day at work? Is it after a disappointment? Is it to forget a loss or pain?" God wants to be the source you seek when you are going through those things. I am a living, breathing witness that no addiction is more powerful than a made-up mind. Partner with God, and all things are possible. Be free, my friends.

Daily Prayer

God, today help me to lay aside every weight that could so easily cause me to stumble. Remind me that addictions are only learned habits, and I can be free of every one of them. Today I choose to live free and be free. In Jesus's name, Amen.

Scripture Reference

Blessed [happy, spiritually prosperous, favored by God] is the man who is steadfast under trial and perseveres when tempted; for when he has passed the test and been approved, he will receive the [victor's] crown of life which the Lord has promised to those who love Him. Let no one say when he is tempted, "I am being tempted by God" [for temptation does not originate from God, but from our own flaws]; for God cannot be tempted by [what is] evil, and He Himself tempts no one. (James 1:12–13 Amplified Bible)

Self-Reflection

What best friend are you ready to break up with?

_____

_____

_____

_____

_____

_____

_____

_____

_____

_____

_____

_____

_____

Day 8

ROTTEN BANANAS

 WHEN I WAS A LITTLE girl, my great-grandmother made the best banana pudding. She would buy bananas and put them in the window to "ripen," as she would say. I can remember watching those bananas each day growing more and more brown. "Grandma, these bananas are rotten. We can't make banana pudding from these." I was so disappointed; my mouth was so ready for that banana pudding.

"They are just about ready," she would reassure me. "Just wait and see!" She wasn't bothered one bit by my impatience and complaints. Sure enough, with the fruit flies swarming around the ripened bananas, she would take them and begin creating the most mouth-watering, greatest banana pudding in the world. I would watch her as she carefully measured and added all the ingredients as if she was creating a masterpiece. Once it was done, I would take a spoonful. I could never figure out how in the world those fly-swarmed bananas could make something taste so good.

I think about our lives and the things we have been through. Some areas of our lives are like those rotten bananas. The stench of the situation has flies swarming all around it. People can smell the stench by our funky, horrible attitudes. We are bitter, angry, resentful, and frankly, we just stink. But God, but God makes all things new. He is able to remake, remodel, redo, revive, rejuvenate our lives. He will make it like it never happened. Do you know God is able to turn our rotten bananas into the best banana pudding you have ever tasted? People will look at you and assume you have never been through hard times. They will see your life and wonder how come you are so blessed. They will never know you once had flies swarming over the rotten areas of your heart.

Daily Prayer

God, today remind me that you make all things new. I will not be embarrassed about my past; it is my testimony and proof that you are a redeemer. In Jesus's name, Amen.

Scripture Reference

Then He who sat on the throne said, "Behold, I make all things new." And He said to me, "Write, for these words are true and faithful." (Revelation 21:5 New King James Version)

Self-Reflection

What areas can God make new for you?

_____

_____

_____

_____

_____

_____

_____

_____

_____

_____

_____

_____

_____

_____

_____

_____

Day 9

SUPERGLUE

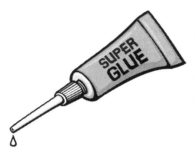

"MOM, I ACCIDENTALLY BROKE YOUR statue on the dining room table," my oldest son confessed to me. "But I got some superglue and fixed it. You can hardly tell it was broken." I looked at my beloved statue, which I received as recognition for my hard work, and immediately saw the crack. *It's ruined,* I thought as I examined every detail of the statue. My son looked at me with anticipation to see how I would respond.

What's funny is every time my son breaks something, he will immediately go into repair mode. Superglue is his first go-to and then duct tape. After I get past the initial anger, I am amazed to see how his mind works. He believes superglue can restore all things as if they were new. My thoughts went to God and how he is the superglue for everything broken in my life. He carefully picks me up, all my broken pieces, strategically and carefully placing everything back together.

The difference between God's superglue and store-bought superglue is you can no longer see where the broken pieces were. I am made completely new, as if it never happened! Even better than I was before. Has life broken you? Do you have pieces scattered from relationships, friends, hurts, disappointments, betrayals, or regrets? Allow the master superglue artist to put you back together. Your life will never be the same!

Daily Prayer

God, today I submit to you the areas in my life where I am broken. I confess where I am still angry, bitter, jealous, and resentful because of things that have happened to me. Father, I allow you to come to me with your spiritual superglue to put me back together again. In Jesus's name, Amen.

Scripture Reference

God, pick up the pieces. Put me back together again. You are my praise! (Jeremiah 17:14 The Message Bible)

Self-Reflection

Where do you need some spiritual superglue?

_____

_____

_____

_____

_____

_____

_____

_____

_____

_____

_____

_____

_____

_____

Day 10

THE TREADMILL

WHEN I GO TO THE gym, my routine is to spend forty-five minutes to an hour on the treadmill. I make sure my phone and headphones are fully charged. I normally listen to music, watch a message, or catch up on shows I may have missed during the week. As I walk, the treadmill tracks my calories, heart rate, and distance. Some days I walk as far as three miles, other days, not so far. No matter how far the treadmill says I have traveled, when the time expires, I am still in the same place I started. I have not gone anywhere! There are some treadmills that have scenery, as if you are actually walking along a country road or mountain trail. But the reality is, you are still exactly where you started.

When this thought first came to my mind, I thought, *How deceiving is that!* You think you have gone somewhere only to find you are in the same place you were when you started. How often have we thought we have overcome a situation, an obstacle, or a person only to find out when something happens, we respond the same way; we react to that person the same way, or we keep doing the same old, bad habits. It is discouraging. "I can't believe I acted like that." "I can't believe I let them back into my life." "I can't believe I am still struggling with this." "I thought I was over this." In reality, my friend, our road to healing and maintaining our healing or deliverance from a person, place, attitude, or thing is much like the treadmill. It is a daily walk, a walk where we constantly have to do a checkup. As we walk on the treadmill of life,

God monitors our heart rates; he ensures we are balanced, not going too fast or too slow. He will also check our spiritual calories to see if we are doing our work to get rid of the excess fat and unproductive things in our lives. But God's treadmill is much different from the earthly one. When we finish our daily walk on God's treadmill, we have moved a great distance. We have advanced. We are in a different place!

Daily Prayer

God, today as I walk on your treadmill, remind me that I am on a spiritual journey with you. I may not feel like I am changing or getting better, but I am. Help me to stay the course. In Jesus's name, Amen.

Scripture Reference

Keep steady my steps according to your promise, and let no iniquity get dominion over me. (Psalm 119:133 English Standard Version)

Self-Reflection

What spiritual journey are you on?

_____

_____

_____

_____

_____

_____

_____

_____

_____

_____

_____

_____

_____

_____

$\mathcal{D}ay\ 11$

CAMOUFLAGE

WHEN I WAS ON ACTIVE duty, our everyday uniform was camouflage print. During times of war, soldiers wear camouflage to hide in plain sight. The chameleon's natural protection is its ability to blend in with its environment. If the environment is blue, it will transition to that color. Brown, the same, and so forth. As a soldier in time of war, your life depends on your ability to remain still so the enemy does not detect you, or to remain focused so you can detect the enemy hiding in plain sight. If you are distracted in time of war, you will walk right up on the enemy, and by the time you realize it, it is too late. *Wikipedia* defines "camouflage" as the use of any combination of materials, coloration, or illumination for concealment, either by making animals or objects hard to see or by disguising them as something else. Another definition is actions or devices intended to disguise or mislead.

I began to think about how the enemy of one's walk with God uses camouflage. In Ezekiel, the Bible tells us that the enemy is full of wisdom. He is not a dumb adversary. He is cunning and conniving, and he hides in plain sight. He hides in the issues and matters of our hearts. When we are not focused, he is able to infiltrate our homes, our relationships, our lives, and eventually our hearts. His infiltration begins subtly in our thoughts. We begin to have judgmental thoughts about a situation, a person, our jobs, our children, our spouses, our church leaders. Thoughts like, *I am the only one working around here. I get sick and tired of picking up after these kids. They want me to do my job and everybody else's in this place. They're always asking for money. I'm getting sick and tired of everybody else in this job moving up but me. She gets on my last nerve. I can't stand her. I will never forgive him for what he did to me. Who asked you, anyway? Mind your own business. I'm not happy in this relationship anymore. We have grown apart. Nobody understands.* These are toxic thoughts that will corrupt any situation or relationship. As we dwell on these toxic thoughts, they begin to be reflected in our actions. We would rather stay home than fellowship. We find reasons to do things alone. We justify our behavior, never realizing it's the enemy in camouflage. He is making us think it's the people on our jobs, it's the people in our churches, it's our spouses, it's our children. All along, it's him, hiding in plain sight.

The ultimate goal in war is to divide and conquer your enemy. It works in sports; if you can get a team to argue and fight, they will be ineffective on the field. It is the same way in our lives, in our relationships, and in our churches. It is the same way in our thoughts toward each other as well. When they are not pure, we will be ineffective in our prayers for others and in our discernment of when someone needs help. By the time we see who the real enemy is, it is too late. We have destroyed our relationships with our words and with our actions. Thank God that he is always with us to guide us, to direct us, and to counsel us when we seek him. He knows the plan of the enemy is to kill, to steal, and to destroy, but he came that we may have life and have it more abundantly. Aren't you ready for the abundant life? Aren't you tired of being misled, misguided, distracted, led astray, used as a puppet, tossed and turned by every wind that blows, being unstable in all your ways? Aren't you tired of being sick and tired?

Daily Prayer

God, today I pray for eyes to see and ears to hear what you are saying to me regarding every area of my life. I thank you that you know all things. I thank you for your precious Holy Spirit—who is my confidante, my counselor, and my friend—who will guide me into all knowledge as I become closer to you. Thank you for a desire to be closer to you. In Jesus's name I pray, Amen.

Scripture Reference

Keep a cool head. Stay alert. The Devil is poised to pounce and would like nothing better than to catch you napping. Keep your guard up. You're not the only ones plunged into these hard times. It's the same with Christians all over the world. So, keep a firm grip on the faith. The suffering won't last forever. It won't be long before this generous God who has great plans for us in Christ—eternal and glorious plans they are!—will have you put together and on your feet for good. He gets the last word; yes, he does. (1 Peter 5:8-11 The Message Bible)

Self-Reflection

How did this chapter resonate with you?

$\mathcal{D}ay\ 12$

TIMBERLAND BOOTS

WHEN STEVE AND I WERE newly married, our oldest son, Reginald, came to live with us. As a new wife and a new stepmother, I tried really hard to get Reginald to like me. He was a young teenager at the time who did not need or want a second mother. In addition, he did not want to share his dad with anyone else.

I remember our first Christmas together as a family. I spent way too much time trying to find the perfect gift for Reginald. I searched and searched. One day, about a week before Christmas, I found the perfect gift. It was a very expensive pair of Timberland Boots. They were the classic brown, high-top boot. They were perfect in every way! I could not wait to give them to Reginald. I wrapped them to perfection. *Oh, he is going to love these!* I thought. I just knew this would improve our relationship. At the time, we were both competing for his dad's time and attention, and, quite frankly, neither of us was winning.

On Christmas morning, Reginald excitedly opened his gifts. As I waited anxiously for him to get to the "perfect gift," my anticipation grew. Finally, he was opening my gift to him. He was a little hesitant at first, but then he tore open the wrapping to reveal the Timberland Boots box. "Timberlands!" he yelled. "My own Timberlands! Oh man! Oh yeah!" He was so excited. I was so excited. I had impressed Reginald! I was proudly patting myself on the back until the moment he tried them on. They did not fit! He tried to put his feet in them, and they didn't fit. All the air left the room. He tried again and again, but his foot simply would not go into the boot. He checked the box for the size. It was size 10, which was his size. "They don't fit," he said disappointedly.

I think I was more disappointed than he was because, after all, this was my chance to win him over. "What do you mean they don't fit?" I yelled. "They are your size. You are doing that on purpose. Let me see. Try them on again!" I was not about to let this little boy show me up. He was going to get his foot inside that shoe even if I had to shove it in there myself. He tried again and again and again and again. The shoes simply did not fit!

Then Steve tried them on. "If he doesn't want them, I will take them," he said as he tried the shoes on. He got them on, but he was walking around in so much pain and agony, they were clearly too small for him as well.

I got even angrier. I don't know why I was so mad. I was being completely selfish. Not once did I even consider how they felt, especially Reginald. "Y'all are both just ungrateful! Just ungrateful," I yelled over and over again. They both stood there in shock, looking puzzled. "Fine," I yelled at them. "I will take them back to the store! See if I ever buy you anything again." I yelled at Reginald. I was taking out all my frustration and disappointment on him. I know none of you have ever done this! LOL! I stormed up to my bedroom, furious because somewhere in my crazy mind, I thought he was doing it on purpose.

About half an hour later, Steve comes upstairs and quietly said, "We figured out the problem. They are a size 10, but a woman's size 10," he explained.

What? I thought. *A woman's size 10? How did I miss that?* I shrunk ten feet in that moment. Not only did I pick the wrong shoe size, I just yelled and screamed at Reginald for something that was completely not his fault. I felt awful and stupid and like the smallest human on the face of the earth. I sat there in silence. Steve had a smirk on his face, and so did Reginald. They were laughing. I felt like they were laughing at me. I felt like even our dog was laughing at me. In my mind, I heard them laughing and saying, "Who goes and buys the wrong shoe! You have to be the dumbest person in the world." Anger welled up in me again and I yelled, "Reginald, I'm sorry," and slammed the door. Not my finest moment.

Has this ever happened to you? Have you ever played a moment in your mind from beginning to end? You know what you are going to say. You know what they are going to say. You see their reaction in your private movie. They are responding exactly how you want them to respond. Everything is perfect in your movie. There are no individuals in your movie. There are only actors and actresses who do exactly what you tell them to do and when you tell them to do it. They say only what you tell them to say and how you tell them to say it. Then, when the real-life moment happens, it is nothing like the way you imagined. But instead of owning up to your feelings and your disappointment, you blame them. No? Just me? Okay. Well, to those people in other countries who have experienced this, I say own up to your feelings. Swallow your pride and muster up a heartfelt, "I'm sorry. I messed up. My bad," whatever you say. Then dust yourself off and keep it moving. One piece of advice: Allow your loved ones to play their own parts in your movie, and just roll with it.

Daily Prayer

God, today help me to always be willing to say a heartfelt, "I'm sorry." Help me to always own up to my mistakes and not try to shift the blame to someone else. In Jesus's name, Amen.

Scripture Reference

"Therefore, confess your sins to one another [your false steps, your offenses], and pray for one another, that you may be healed and restored. The heartfelt and persistent prayer of a righteous man (believer) can accomplish much [when put into action and made effective by God—it is dynamic and can have tremendous power]. (James 5:16 Amplified Bible)

Self-Reflection

Is there someone you need to apologize to? Go do it.

_____

_____

_____

_____

_____

_____

_____

_____

_____

_____

_____

_____

_____

_____

_____

Day 13

ARE YOU KIDDING ME?

HAVE YOU EVER WOKEN UP and from the minute you stepped out of bed, you felt the day was just dead set against you? For example, you wake up and the shirt or tie or dress you were going to wear that day has a stain on it that you didn't see when you laid it out. Or you can't find the tie that matches your shirt perfectly. Or for some reason, your socks are matched incorrectly. There is no toothpaste! No clean towels! The kids are moving slowly and screaming at each other for no apparent reason. The dog is barking out of control. You made the last cup of coffee the day before, and you remember you forgot to buy more just as you are looking for the coffee can. Everything is chaotic.

I recently had that day. Finally, everyone was loaded in the car. I was running late, the kids were going to be late if I didn't leave in the next minute, and just as I closed and locked the front door, I heard the kids yell, "Mom, get the car keys!"

"Are you kidding me? Why are you in the car without the keys?" Panic came over me until I remembered the hidden spare key. I got the spare key, opened the door, grabbed the car keys, and like a madwoman determined to get the kids to school on time and me to work on time, I flew into the car.

As I am driving, I couldn't understand why everyone else on the road did not realize the rush I was in. They were just coasting along, following the speed limit with smiles on their faces. I even see some drivers singing! Are you kidding me? Singing! I wanted to yell at them. I wanted to tell them about my morning! What was wrong with them? Couldn't they just get out of my way? Move! As I was yelling at the people in the other cars, I caught a glimpse of my children. The looks on their faces were a mixture of terror and surprise. In that moment, I snapped back to my senses. I began to hear my heart talk to me: *Erin, is it really that serious? Is it the end of the world if the kids are late? If you are late? What is more important, getting there full of stress or getting there peacefully and safely? Or even worse, an accident that could harm you or the children? Calm down, take a deep breath. It is okay. And if it is not okay, so what?* I felt a sense of peace come over me. I looked back at the kids and announced, "Who wants McDonalds? We are going to be late, so we might as well make the most of it!"

Daily Prayer

Lord, today help me not take life so seriously. Remind me to find pleasure in the small things and not allow little molehills to turn into mountains. Help me to remember that it is all in my attitude. Remind me to always ask you for help when I am overwhelmed and stressed. In Jesus's name, Amen.

Scripture Reference

God is good a hiding place in tough times. He recognizes and welcomes anyone looking for help, No matter how desperate the trouble. (Nahum 1:7 Message Bible)

Self-Reflection

In what ways do you find yourself overreacting?

_____

_____

_____

_____

_____

_____

_____

_____

_____

_____

_____

_____

_____

_____

Day 14

MASSAGE THERAPY

A FEW YEARS AGO, MY husband blessed me with a membership for a monthly massage. Throughout the years, I have gone in for a feel-good massage, mild pressure, not deep tissue. I didn't want to feel any discomfort during my massage, just a relaxing, feel-good massage. Well, the last couple of months, I have been stressed out over several things: family, children, career, sales, numbers, clients, church; the list goes on and on. I decided I needed a massage. This particular appointment, I told the therapist I was under a lot of stress and needed her to focus on the areas where I was holding stress in my body. She asked me if I wanted mild pressure or firm, deep-tissue pressure. Now, keep in mind I have always elected the mild pressure, but this particular day, I said, "Firm. I really need to be relieved of all this stress."

As the therapist began to work out the areas of tightness in my shoulders, back, and neck, I began to feel very uncomfortable. The pain was at times unbearable! Very uncomfortable! I wanted to stop her and say, "You know, can you ease up a bit?" But I didn't. I knew the only way to get rid of the built-up stress in my body was to allow her to continue.

She would say from time to time, "How is that pressure? Just let me know if it is too much." I would reply in a very unconvincing voice, "I am fine." As she continued the massage, whenever the pressure was unbearable, I would take a deep breath and exhale slowly. In and then out, in and then out, in and then out.

As she continued, my mind went to the Holy Spirit and my walk with the Lord. I began to think about the things in my life I had allowed to build up in my heart and in my mind and in my emotions. I thought of the things I was stressed out about. I thought about the areas where things had happened in my life and I'd stopped because the pain or the discipline of it was just too much for me to bear. I thought about the areas I had asked God to focus on in my life, but when the pain was too unbearable, I pulled back or asked him to lighten up. *God,* I thought, *I understand now. You were trying to work things out of my life that were not good for me. Relationships that were toxic. Jobs that were not part of my destiny. Habits that were slowly killing me. From this point on, I will stay on your massage table. I will not ask you to ease up. I will lie there and take it. I will breathe in and out. I will breathe in your ways, your Word, your plans, and your will. And I will breathe out everything that tries to exalt itself against you, especially me. God, you are the ultimate massage therapist, and when you are finished with me, I will be all that you created me to be for your glory.*

Daily Prayer

Lord, today I commit to you those areas of my life I have been unwilling to commit. I submit to your will in my life. I will lie on your massage table and allow you to work on the areas where I have built a wall between you and me. I will breathe through the painful moments and trust you with all my heart. In Jesus's name, Amen.

Scripture Reference

Yet you, Lord, are our Father. We are the clay; you are the potter; we are all the work of your hand. (Isaiah 64:8 New International Version)

Self-Reflection

What are some areas where you need to apply pressure and change?

_____

_____

_____

_____

_____

_____

_____

_____

_____

_____

_____

_____

_____

_____

_____

_____

$\mathcal{D}ay\ 15$

CLEAVAGE

SOMETIME AGO, WE FOUND OURSELVES out of church and unconnected to a local church body. Our family was struggling in all areas, communication, careers, and in our marriage. We were out in the world by ourselves, without any spiritual leadership. Around this time, my husband and I were really going through some things and on a fast train to divorce court. He did not want to talk to anyone about it, not any of his closest friends or the people he saw as spiritual leaders. One day Steve saw one of the leaders of a church we had previously visited at a store and asked them to pray for us. He said we were going through a rough time in our marriage, and we needed help. Shortly after that, Steve and I began to meet with them on a weekly basis and started to get the help we needed. Needless to say, we became members of their church. There was no doubt in our minds we were meant to be at that particular church and at that particular time in our lives. That is, until, "cleavage" showed up.

I had gained a lot of weight, well over thirty pounds, from depression. I was struggling with low self-esteem and desperately wanted to be noticed by my husband. This one particular Sunday, I found a dress that he liked to see me in. I put it on, but because I had gained so much weight, my breasts were noticeably bulging out. But I wore it anyway. The minute I walked into the church, my cleavage was noticed. I was repeatedly told to cover it up and to get a pin. I felt judged and insulted.

At that moment, it was like the spirit of offense walked right into my mind, sat down, crossed its legs. and began to talk to me. The negative thoughts began to play in my mind, and it went something like this. *Really? Is this how people are treated in church now? No wonder people don't come to church. Who do church people think they are? They don't know you like that. You are not supposed to treat people like that! Those are people's rules. God accepts you just as you are. You should just walk out right now. If I were you, I wouldn't stay here another minute.*

Offense went on and on, so much so, I cannot tell you what the sermon was about that day. Steve looked over at me; he could tell I was near tears from embarrassment, and with no compassion in his voice asked, "You offended, huh?" The tears welled up in my eyes and began to roll down my checks.

I was offended. My feelings were hurt. I went home that day unsure if I was going to return. Offense had pled his case and was winning the popular vote.

In my heart, I began to talk to Daddy God about how I felt. I explained my reason for not wanting to go back to that church. I pled my case and justified my actions and feelings. He simply asked me, "Do you believe I sent you there?" *Yes, but,* I thought. "No buts, if you believe I sent you there, are you going to allow one person to remove you from a place I sent you? Look at how much you have grown since you have been there. Look at the progress you have made in your relationship. This is just another area where you need to grow. You knew that dress was inappropriate for church when you put it on, but you wore it anyway. And that is not her fault." I began to cry as offense got up and walked out of my heart. I had almost allowed offense to move me from my place of assignment and blessing. The next time I saw that person, she apologized, but I had already realized it was not about her at all. It was about me and how I reacted.

Today, those leaders are important people in our lives. God uses them to instruct us, correct us, pray for us, challenge us, and provoke us to move into our callings in life. Spiritual leaders and pastors are key people God uses to help us grow, and they watch over our souls. Every interaction with pastors and spiritual leaders will not be comfortable and enjoyable. If they are true leaders, they will correct and challenge you to be what you were created to be.

In what ways have you allowed offense to move you from a place of blessing or assignment? What about from a job or career? A relationship? Offense is a tool that the enemy uses to steal, kill, and destroy God's plans for our lives. He uses people, circumstances, and situations to hurt us. We get offended and stay offended. We allow bitterness to set up in our hearts, unpack its bags, and move in for good. Recognize offense for what it is. It wants to rob you of God's divine purpose and will for your life. Offense is not your friend. It does not have your best interests at heart.

I learned during this situation that when offenses come, it has more to do with how I respond and react to them rather than the offense or the person committing the offense. But too often, we get it twisted. We focus on the offense and the person. Therefore, we get stuck and stagnant. Offense will keep us paralyzed and ineffective.

Offense tried to rob me of the blessings God had for me at that appointed time and place in my life. Now I am not going anywhere until God says so. What about you?

Note: If you find yourself focusing more on the offense then the message of this day, please reread this chapter until the point becomes clear.

Daily Prayer

Lord, today I release all who have offended me. God, I pray that you restore all that I have lost because of allowing "offense" to move into my heart and cause me to move without your permission or blessing. Help me to realize that offenses will come, but it is how I respond and react to them that may cause me to stumble. God, I pray that the next time offense knocks at my door, I will not let it in, but I will bring it to you. In your Son, Jesus's name, Amen.

Scripture Reference

Great peace have they which love your law: and nothing shall offend them. (Psalm 119:165 King James Version)

Self-Reflection

How have you been offended? It is time to forgive.

_____

_____

_____

_____

_____

_____

_____

_____

_____

_____

_____

_____

_____

$\mathcal{D}ay$ *16*

DUNCAN

MY FIRST ENCOUNTER WITH DUNCAN was not a pretty one. We had decided to send our oldest son to a military reform high school, like a boot camp for teenagers. The day of orientation we were waiting outside when I noticed what appeared to be an argument. It was a woman and a young man. I got out of my car and approached them. As I approached, I heard the young man yelling obscenities at the woman. As I got closer, I discovered she was his mother. He was calling her all sorts of names and railing insults. He told her he wished she would die. The words were spoken with such anger and rage that my heart sank. He tried to slam the car door on his mother, and then he spit on her! I was shocked and appalled. I could tell she was afraid of him. I immediately intervened. I asked, "What is going on? What is wrong?" The mother explained she told her son that if he didn't go into the program, he could not return home with her. She wanted him to get out of the car, or she was calling the police. She went on to explain how his father had died, and her son blamed her for his passing. She said things were not the same since his father died, and he was angry all the time. She said he threatened her and her other son. She said he was dangerous, and she had called the police on him several times. My heart went out to her. I could feel her pain, her fear, all of it. I looked at Duncan and asked him, "Do you know what the Bible says about your father and mother? Do you know that if you honor your father and your mother, your days will be long on the earth, and it will be well with you?"

He looked at me in disgust and asked, "Oh, is this what we are going to do now?"

I replied, "Yes, this is what we are going to do right now." I began to pray for him. I began to pray against the spirit of anger. I began to speak boldly over him.

He said, "Look, if you stop, I will go into the building." He got out of the car, and they went into the building. I got back into my car.

I could not get Duncan off my mind. So much so that I began to pray for him and his mother. I asked God to show himself to Duncan. I prayed that he would learn about Jesus. A few weeks later, our son Judah entered the program. For the first two weeks, we did not hear from him. The day he called, after asking him how he was and how was it going, I asked about Duncan. "Judah, remember that boy, Duncan? Did he get in?"

He said, "No, Mom. He did not get in. They did not let him in."

After that phone call, I prayed for Duncan even more. There were nights I would wake up thinking about him, and I would just pray for him. I could see his face. I could see his mother's face. I asked God to protect them. I begged God not to allow the devil to have Duncan. I prayed against anger, bitterness, resentment, and rage. I asked God to heal Duncan's heart. I asked God to restore his relationship with his mother. I asked God to help him to forgive his mother. I prayed and prayed and prayed. I was convinced I would never see Duncan again, but that did not stop me from praying for him. It was like he was my son, and I was not going to stop praying for him.

Fast-forward five and half months. We were at graduation, and the 144 cadets were lined up to receive their certificates of completion, awards, and accolades. As we waited on our son to walk across the stage, I heard the name Duncan _____. That name got my attention, and as I looked up, I saw Duncan's picture on the screen. I heard, "With honors, Duncan _____." I looked at my mother, who was sitting next to me. "That's Duncan. That's Duncan! I have been praying for that boy." Tears welled up in my eyes as I saw "my" Duncan walk across the stage to receive his graduation certificate with honors. Not only did he receive his graduation certificate, he received three cash scholarships. I was so proud of him, just like I was of my own son.

My heart filled with gratitude as I thought of my Daddy God. He didn't have to allow me to see my prayers manifested like that. He allowed me to see my prayers answered and to witness Duncan's success in the program. He graduated with honors, and on top of everything else, there were scholarships for him. *Wow, God,* I thought. *Thank you for allowing me to see this. Thank you for allowing me to see my prayers answered. Thank you! Thank you! Thank you!*

Today, allow me to encourage you. I don't know who you are praying for. I don't know what situation you are trusting God to turn around. I don't know what has you up day and night. I don't know what is heavy on your heart. Your marriage, your child, your mother, your father, your brother, your sister, aunt, uncle, friend, job, disease, sickness, addiction, whatever it may be, don't stop praying. Don't stop believing! Don't stop interceding. Don't give up. You may need to scream. You may need to shout. But don't you give up! It may be one month, six months, years before you see the manifestation of your prayers, but I can promise you this; you will see your prayers answered! If he did it for me, he will do it for you. He has no respect of person.

Daily Prayer

Dear Lord, I pray a stick-to-itiveness over my sisters and brothers. God, you know the thing they have been praying and believing in you for. God, just like you allowed me to see my prayers answered, do it for them. Allow them to see their prayers answered. Allow them to see your glory in whatever the situation may be. Do it now, God, in your Son Jesus's name, Amen.

Scripture Reference

That's why I urge you to pray for absolutely everything, ranging from small to large. Include everything as you embrace this God-life, and you'll get God's everything. (Mark 11:24 The Message Bible)

Self-Reflection

Please share a time when God answered your prayer. He is the same God!

_____

_____

_____

_____

_____

_____

_____

_____

_____

_____

_____

_____

_____

_____

$\mathcal{D}ay\ 17$

DOMINOS

SINCE JOINING THE NAVY IN 1988, I have enjoyed playing the game of dominos. During liberty time, we would spend time playing cards, dominos, and drinking. We talked trash and just had a good time. Once I retired in 2012, the opportunities I had to play dominos were fewer and fewer. A couple of years ago, I got invited to the online domino community. Thousands of people from all over the world, from different walks of life, most of who were not Christian, played against each other through a domino app, kind of like an adult version of video games. In the beginning, it was like old times, playing and beating people, talking trash, playing in tournaments, and winning. I began to spend more and more time playing online dominos. If I was in a tournament, I had to make sure I made a play within twenty-four hours, or I would forfeit the game.

The hobby began to cut into my sleep time, my family time, my work time. I spent hours upon hours playing online dominos. If I was in the middle of a game and someone interrupted me— like my children, my husband, a phone call from a client—I was instantly aggravated, and my responses were short and layered with impatience. My children started to make comments like, "Let me guess, dominos?" "Mom, did you hear what I said?" Even my husband grew bothered by the amount of time I spent playing online dominos. I didn't care. I was good at it, and I liked playing dominos. I would justify my behavior. I thought, *I don't bother him about his hobbies, and the minute I get something I enjoy doing, here he come with some drama. Now he knows what it feels like to be ignored.*

This went on for years. Then one day, God began to talk to me about it. I began to see that although this domino app and online community of players was not a bad thing, I had allowed it to consume me and to become an idol in my life. It was more important to me than work or spending time with my children and my husband. It was more important to me than God, because the time I used to spend with God, I now spent checking my domino app to see if my opponent had made a move. If my opponent was online at the same time I was, it would take us twenty to thirty minutes to play the game out, sometimes causing me to be late for work. The time I used to spend in my car driving, reviewing, and listening to the message my pastor preached on Sunday, I was driving and trying to make plays on the domino app. This thing had a hold on me, and I was not going to be able to get out of it without the help of God. I finally began to listen to my family and to the Lord.

I knew the domino game had to go. Now I know many of you have never struggled with anything like this. I know you can play Candy Crush or Words with Friends for thirty minutes and put it down without hesitation. I know you only spend a few minutes on Facebook a day, and then you are done with it. I know you don't spend hours on your Twitter and Instagram accounts to see how the rich and famous are living, who they are married to, divorced from, what they wore to the awards show, or their latest performances. I know you are not glued to the television for hours on end. I know you have everything in your life in its place, and nothing is out of order. But to those of us who are not as strong as the rest of you, who have allowed things to creep into our lives and begin to suck the life out of our important relationships, I offer this prayer to you.

Daily Prayer

Lord, in ways and areas where I have removed you as Lord and King and put people and things in your place, I repent and turn away from those people and things that have taken time away from you and my important relationships. I repent for wasting time in areas that are not adding to my life, my relationships, or your kingdom. I put you back on the throne of my heart and my life, never to be removed again. In Jesus's name, Amen.

Scripture Reference

You must not have any other God but me. (Exodus 20:3 New Living Translation)

Self-Reflection

What are some habits you should stop? What are you waiting for?

_____

_____

_____

_____

_____

_____

_____

_____

_____

_____

_____

_____

_____

_____

Day 18

My New Hairdo

I LOVE EXPERIMENTING WITH NEW hairdos. I can look through a magazine, scroll through Facebook, or watch television and see a style that I find really appealing. I begin to imagine myself with that hairdo. I see myself walking into a room as heads turn and people smile. I see myself walking into a meeting, and people are just breathless from the way I look. Not to mention my husband. Oh, I just know he will love it. Then I go on a quest to find the right hair. I save the picture for my stylist because she will need it to get me to look exactly like the woman in the picture. I am determined that my hair will look just like that! I have seen myself in my imagination, and I look good with this hairdo. No one can tell me differently.

As my dream starts to come together, I have the hair, I have the appointment, and I set out to the beauty shop. My mind plays over and over again how people will respond once I walk in the room, especially my husband. Oh, he will not be able to keep his hands off me! I get myself all psyched up. As I sit in the stylist's chair, she and I talk endlessly about how cute the style is. She tells me over and over again, "Girl, this is you. This is too cute! You are going to work this hairdo!" We giggle and laugh as we envision the reactions. After three to four hours at the beauty shop, the masterpiece is done. She hands me the mirror, and I am breathtaking! I mean, I look good. The hairdo is perfect. It fits me perfectly. My excitement is bursting. Oooh wee, I look good! I add the finishing touches: my earrings, my makeup, and my favorite lipstick with a little gloss to make my lips pop. I hug my beautician and rush out of the shop. As I drive home,

I replay over and over my husband's reaction and those of the people at the office when I show up at work on Monday. "Oooh, can't touch this!" I got the MC Hammer anointing going on in my head, and I laugh.

I pull in the driveway of my home, and I can't turn the car off quickly enough. I take one last look in the rearview mirror and wink at myself, "Girl, you are too cute," I say to myself as I get out of the car. I walk into the house and the kids greet me. "What have you done to your hair?" they yell.

My youngest, who is so much like her father, screams, "Is that some more weave?"

"Yes," I reply. "Do you like it?"

"Yes, Mom. It's pretty," she says as she reaches up to touch my hair.

"Where is your dad?" I am so excited to see his reaction I can hardly contain myself. I walk into the room where he is sitting and look at his face. He looks up and says nothing. I mean nothing! He takes a few seconds' pause, which in my mind is one second too long. "That's different. I mean, it's okay," he finally responds. My bubble instantly bursts, and the air slowly leaves my body. I thank him and go to my bedroom, disappointment welling up in me. My eyes start to tear up. *Different?* I think. *What does that mean? Different? Okay?*

Now, please allow me to be completely transparent, this used to knock the wind out of me. My husband's opinion weighed heavily on things in my life. If he didn't like it, I didn't like it. If he had a negative opinion about something, I had a negative opinion about it, especially myself. I allowed my self-worth to be caught up in how he treated me, responded to me, and loved me. But then God did something. He began to talk to me about idols. And he showed me how I made an idol out of my husband. My husband's opinion was more important to me than what God said about me, and God was not having that! He began to rebuild my self-esteem. He began to reaffirm what he said about me and to help me see myself as he saw me. He showed me true beauty comes from how I felt about myself, not the opinions of others, even my husband. Now when I get a new hairdo and everything about the situation is exactly the same, I tell myself something like, "Something is seriously wrong with that man. Doesn't he know cute when it is staring him right in the face?" I look at myself in the mirror, wink at myself, and I keep it moving. I wear my new hairdo with so much confidence and with the glow of Jesus shining through me. Now there are days when my husband looks at me and says, "You are absolutely beautiful." In my mind, I think, *It took you long enough to realize it.* The really funny thing about that response is I am not talking to him; I am talking to myself.

Daily Prayer

Today, Lord, help me to appreciate the gift of me. Everything about me you patiently designed and created. You picked my eyes, my ears, my lips, my legs, my figure, my personality, my smile, and my temperament. And when you finished making the masterpiece of me, you called me "Unique," you called me "Wonderfully Made." You called me your child, and you put a stamp of approval on me and said I was good! In Jesus's name, Amen.

Scripture Reference

I will praise you because I have been remarkably and wondrously made. Your works are wondrous, and I know this very well. (Psalm 139:14 Christian Standard Bible)

Self-Reflection

In what area are you more concerned about what people say than God?

_____

_____

_____

_____

_____

_____

_____

_____

_____

_____

_____

_____

_____

$\mathcal{D}ay\ 19$

SPIT SHOESHINE

 AFTER SPENDING TWENTY-FOUR YEARS IN the military, one thing I knew how to do was shine a boot. To be honest, I was not very good at it in the beginning. I had to learn the basics. I can remember as a little girl, watching my granddaddy get dressed. He always grabbed his shoeshine brush and brushed his Stacy Adams a couple of times, and then he was ready.

When I joined the Navy in 1988, I quickly learned that one or two brushes across my boots was not going to pass inspection. I learned that in order to get a reflection in your boot so glossy you could see yourself in it, you had to spend hours establishing a solid base. That base was formed with spit, water, an old cloth (usually an old T-shirt), and shoe polish. To start, you had to wrap that cloth tightly around your two forefingers and dab them into the shoe polish and then the water. At first, you needed a lot of polish to get a solid, smooth base. As you rubbed that polish into the leather of the boot, it remained dull with no sign of a shine. Hours upon hours, I spent on my boots: polish, water, rub. It had to be in that order: polish, water, rub; polish, water, rub; polish, water, rub. If the cloth began to get a layer on it that kept it from distributing the polish evenly on the boot, I found a clean spot on the rag and continued my process—polish, water, rub; polish, water, rub. As I rubbed, I would begin to see a shine. However, that shine was not one in which I could see my reflection. So I continued the process: polish, water, rub; polish, water, rub; polish, water, rub. Hours passed as I continued the process. My bootcamp Company Commander, Chief

Petty Officer Jones, the person who oversaw my transition from civilian life to military life and the one responsible for turning me into a military member said, "You are almost there. It is time for you to add your spit."

"Spit? Now that is just nasty," I objected.

"It is, but your spit has a natural chemical in it to bring out the shine. Trust me. Try it," he encouraged me.

Sure enough, I spit on my cloth and began to rub that spit into the leather. The more I rubbed, the shinier the boot became. I got excited! "Chief, it's working!" I yelled.

"I told you," he replied. I continued with the special ingredient, my spit, and it wasn't long before I could see my reflection in my boot, right down to my teeth.

As I write this, I think of us as the boot and how God uses the polish, water, and spit to bring out his reflection in us. As we move through this world, we are in the process of becoming more and more like Jesus. The process is sometimes redundant. Sometimes we wonder how long this will take. How long will I have to stay at this job? When is my son going to get it right? When am I going to get out of debt? Is this sickness going to kill me? But God is adding more polish, more water, and rubbing. More polish, more water, and more rubbing. He uses every situation to bring out his reflection in us. He wants people to see him when they see us. And just when we are about to give up, he adds his spit! Then he rubs us some more, adding more and more of his spit. We start to become more and more like him. His reflection is us, and we are him. His ways are our ways. His words are our words. We are truly his children and his disciples. All because of some spit!

Daily Prayer

Lord, thank you for your spit, your breath, your Word, your guidance, your correction, your direction, and how you use life and its circumstances to make me more and more like you. In Jesus's name, Amen.

Scripture Reference

And we know [with great confidence] that God [who is deeply concerned about us] causes all things to work together [as a plan] for good for those who love God, to those who are called according to His plan and purpose. (Romans 8:28 Amplified Bible)

Self-Reflection

In what area are you striving to be more like Jesus?

_____

_____

_____

_____

_____

_____

_____

_____

_____

_____

_____

_____

_____

Day 20

Laundry Detergent

A COUPLE DAYS AGO, MY daughters and I went into Dollar General to get a few items. As they always do, the sale signs got my attention. I went up and down the aisles, looking for a good deal. One of the items I needed was laundry detergent. As I went down the aisle where the detergent was, I noticed a sale sign on the brand I normally buy. I read it to say buy three, get one free. *Wow,* I thought, *that is a good deal. Thanks, God!* I loaded my basket with twelve, thinking I was going to pay for nine and get three free. I was so excited. I shopped around some more and went to the line. As the clerk began to ring up my items, I noticed I was not getting the discount. I watched carefully as the clerk finished and gave me my total. I asked, "Did I get my discount for the detergent?"

She responded, "No, ma'am. This happened several times today already. You have to have the online coupon to get the discount."

I was so disappointed. "What? I didn't understand it to be that way. That is so misleading." I began to get upset. "Why would you have a sign up with misleading information? And if it has happened several times today, that should tell you something is wrong with it."

By this time, other people in the line were beginning to take notice. The clerk at the other register chimed in, "It states it clearly on the sign, if you had taken the time to read it!"

Now I was really getting mad as I walked back to the aisle to recheck the sign. Not to mention, people in line, as well as my

78

daughters, were waiting and watching all of this unfold. I could feel heat rising in my neck, and I was really getting angry. When I got to the sign, the rude clerk pointed and said, "See! It says it right there, 'Online coupon needed for the discount.'"

The print was so small I had to squint to see it, but it was there. So now I was really mad, not because I was wrong—well, yes, because I was wrong—but also because this chick felt the need to come point it out, and her delivery was horrible. She did not have to say it like that. I went back to the cash register and as I walked, I told her that the print was so small you needed a microscope to see it. It was misleading, and they needed to take the sign down. "We are not taking it down," she challenged me right back. When I got back to the counter, I told the clerk to remove the items because I didn't want them. She politely took the items off as her counterpart kept glaring at me, and I glared at her. I got my items, and the girls and I walked out of the store.

As I left the store, God said to me, "Erin, why did you act like that? Who did you glorify in there? Will you ever be able to witness to those individuals in that store if I needed you to?"

I felt conviction fill my heart. *No, God,* I thought. *That was all about me and my feelings. It had nothing to do with you. You did not get any glory out of my actions.* I would like to tell you I walked back into that store and apologized. I would like to tell you I later prayed for that young woman and led her to Christ. But I didn't. I missed that opportunity to be a witness for the Lord. Through something so small as laundry detergent, I glorified my emotions instead of God. I failed that What Would Jesus Do? test miserably.

If you can think of times where you have failed the What Would Jesus Do? test, I have some good news! Every day, we get another opportunity to get it right. God's mercies are fresh and new every morning. So today, set yourself up to give God glory, not just with your mouth, but with your life.

Daily Prayer

God, I repent for the times I have fallen short. I repent for when I have failed to glorify you with my life. I will start this day mindful of my actions and words toward other people. I will not be distracted by small and petty things, and I will not allow them to destroy my witness. God, I desire for you to get the glory out of my life more than I desire to be right or justified. In Jesus's name, Amen.

Scripture Reference

Prove by the way you live that you have repented of your sins and turned to God. (Matthew 3:8 New Living Translation)

Do those things that prove you have turned to God and have changed the way you think and act. (God's Word Translation)

Self-Reflection

Share a time when you didn't represent God well.

_____

_____

_____

_____

_____

_____

_____

_____

_____

_____

_____

_____

_____

$\mathcal{D}ay$ 21

THE CHRISTMAS ORNAMENT

STEVE CALLED ME ONE MORNING in total frustration. As he explained, he had just left the school after dropping the kids off. He was on his way back to the house when he received a call from Joi, our eleven-year-old daughter. "Dad, I need the Christmas ornament! We are decorating our class tree today, and I need it by twelve fifteen. Okay, Dad. Thank you. I love you." And she hung up.

Did I mention that the school is a thirty- to forty-minute drive from our home depending on traffic? Not to mention, he was trying to get back before a 9:00 a.m. coaching call. I could hear the aggravation in his voice as he continued to fuss. "She has no regard for what I have to do. She just assumes that I am going to take care of it, no questions asked. She just said, 'Thank you,' and hung up the phone. These kids!"

As he went on and on, my mind went to our Father in heaven. Why don't we have this kind of faith in him? When we ask him for things, we still worry about it. We keep asking him over and over, as if we think he has forgotten what we asked for. We spend hours upon hours, even days, thinking about it, pondering over it because we really don't believe he is going to deliver. We think for some reason he is going to withhold his blessings from us, withhold our healings, withhold our breakthroughs, allow our businesses to fail, not fix our relationships or our broken marriages, not take care of our children. Unlike Joi, who had total confidence in her earthly father, that he was going to deliver. She didn't call him back in ten minutes and ask, "Dad, where are you? Did you go to the store yet? Did you forget about me? Am I not important enough to you to make this happen for me?" She wasn't nagging her dad; she simply believed he was going to deliver. Sure enough, after going to three stores at eight thirty, her dad found some Christmas ornaments! Not only did he find one, he bought an array of ornaments so she could choose which one she liked the best. He is a good father, but our heavenly Father is a good, good Father. If our earthly fathers know how to give good gifts to their children, how much better does our Father in heaven? He will perfect everything that concerns us.

Daily Prayer

Lord, today help me to have childlike faith. Help me to believe in you and not doubt you. Help me to know beyond a shadow of a doubt that you are my good, good Father, and I am loved by you. Help me to be assured that you will take care of me. You desire to supply all my needs according to your riches in glory. In your Son, Jesus's name, Amen.

Scripture Reference

Therefore I tell you, whatever you ask for in prayer, believe that you have received it, and it will be yours. And when you stand praying, if you hold anything against anyone, forgive them, so that your father in heaven may forgive your sins. (Mark 11:24–25 New International Version)

Self-Reflection

Share an area in your life where you desire childlike faith.

_____

_____

_____

_____

_____

_____

_____

_____

_____

_____

_____

_____

_____

_____

Day 22

THE DINING ROOM TABLE

As a young wife, after we moved into our first house, I desperately wanted to fill it with furniture to make it a home. We were in our fifth year of marriage, and our sons, Judah and Josiah, were babies. I wanted a dining room table. I shopped around and found this elaborate dining room table and hutch for five thousand dollars. It was beautiful, top of the line, handcrafted, cherry wood; it was the kind of dining room table you would see in a magazine. Now, at the time, Steve and I were barely making it from paycheck to paycheck. We had not learned how to manage our finances, and we were not making smart choices in our spending. We were very emotional with purchases. If we wanted it, we bought it, and we didn't take the cost into account.

One day, Steve came to me and said God had given him a plan to get us out of debt. He explained the plan and asked for my agreement. Now this dining room table was in no way, shape, or form going to fit into this new get out of debt plan. But I was determined to get that table. Every opportunity I got, I brought it up, and Steve always said no, not right now.

I was so frustrated with him that I went to our pastor, Cheryl Cosey; we call her "Ma" Cosey. I explained my case to her as she sat patiently listening to me. Once I finished, she said, "Erin, I understand you want that table, but God gave him a plan to get you out of debt. As his wife, God designed you to be a helpmate. Ask yourself how you are helping him right now. He is saying not right now, and you keep bringing it up. You can shop around and find a really nice table for right now. Someone is always selling furniture, and you can find some really nice things. You can put the one you really want on the back burner for later, when you can afford it. You never know. In being obedient to God now, when you buy the one you want later, it will probably be cheaper or even maybe on sale!"

This was not what I wanted to hear, but the wisdom that she spoke went directly to my heart. "Okay, Ma Cosey," I said. And I began shopping for a table. I found a four-piece green table with a matching hutch that someone was selling for $150. It was nice, and it fit perfectly in our kitchen. I was satisfied, and so was my husband. We used that table until we left Illinois.

Fast-forward. The plan God gave Steve got us completely out of debt. We moved back to Florida and into our current home. We did some remodeling, and I brought up the dining room table. Steve was in agreement and set aside the $5,000 I needed to purchase the table. I begin searching for the set. I searched and searched, but I could not find it anywhere. I had given up when one day, I walked into a small, local furniture store in my hometown, and there, right in front of my eyes, was my dining room table and hutch for $2,500! I was so excited to see Steve's smile when I shared with him that, not only did I find the table, but it was half of what we budgeted. Call me "helpmate!" Yep, that's my name.

Today, I want to remind you that God's timing is perfect. There may be some material things you want that you have not been able to purchase, a move you are wanting to make, a new job you are contemplating, or a relationship you are considering beginning or even ending. We may never know what God is doing behind the scenes, but if you feel a hesitation for any reason, wait. If you are married and there is no agreement, wait. If you are feeling uneasy, unsure, rushed, anxious, manipulated, or pushed, that means wait. The timing is off, and God wants you to wait. Be obedient to his unction; he has a reason. Unlike humans, God always has our very best interests at heart!

Daily Prayer

Father, I thank you for being my guide, my confidant, my best friend, my counselor, my provider, my lawyer, my everything. You know the plans you have for me, and I admit, I do not. Help me to trust in you with all my heart and not to lean on my own understanding or my own way of doing things. In all my ways, I will acknowledge you, and you will direct my path. In your Son Jesus's name, Amen.

Scripture Reference

The blessing of the Lord makes one rich and he adds no sorrow with it. (Proverbs 10:22 New King James Version)

Self-Reflection

Is there a decision you are contemplating?

$\mathcal{D}ay\ 23$

SPADES

FOR AS LONG AS I can remember, the game spades has been a part of my life. As a little girl, I watched my parents play. It was exciting to watch all the theatrics of the game. The smack talking, the slamming of the cards, and the infamous "Boston."

For those of you who don't know how to play spades, here is a quick explanation. The spade suit is the trump suit. Four players are split into two teams. They are dealt thirteen cards each, and based on the hand they are dealt, they pledge to make a certain number of books. The game is over when the first team reaches five hundred points. For example, if your team bids seven books and gets seven books, you are given seventy points. If you don't make your books, then you are negative seventy. That's called being in the hole or getting set. If you get set, the chance of you winning the game is slim to none—unless, of course, you can set your opponent. If your team gets all thirteen books, that is called a Boston. The game begins as each player follows suit (hearts, diamonds, clubs, spades), and the highest card wins the book. As I said, the spade is the trump card, meaning if you have none of the suit being played, you can play a spade and win the book, no matter how small the spade is. For instance, the deuce of spades can beat the ace of hearts. The game of spades is so popular that there have been apps created so you can play online.

I began to think about God and how he is the ultimate trump card. Spades is similar to whist and bridge, where the trump is

90

defined by the suit (spades, hearts, clubs, or diamonds). Any card in the defined suit wins over a card that is not of that suit. The word "trump" means to outrank or defeat someone or something. As a young female, I made decisions that were just stupid, but God kept me safe. He trumped every bad decision I made. My husband grew up in the projects. His mother drank heavily, and he often had to take care of her as a little boy. Statistically, he should have been in jail or dead by now, but the ultimate trump card stepped into his situation. You may have made mistakes in your life. You may have had a very difficult childhood. You may have been through a tragedy in your life, and by the world's standards and statistics, you should be in a mental institution, disgusted, depressed, or living in regret, but for God! Many are the afflictions of the righteous, but God delivers us from them all! What the enemy meant for evil, God turned into something for your good. When is the last time you reached up and got a dose of God's deliverance? It is his children's bread, you know. I believe the ultimate trump card just showed up in your situation. He just showed up in your emotions. He just showed up in the room you are in right now. Praise him for trumping the situation right now.

Daily Prayer

Father, today I realize that no matter what is happening all around me, you are in control. You ultimately have the last word. You are the trump card in my and my family's lives. In any situation that is important to me, it is important to you. Thank you, God. In Jesus's name, Amen.

Scripture Reference

The righteous person faces many troubles, but the Lord comes to the rescue each time. (Psalm 34:19 English Standard Version)

Self-Reflection

Share an area where you need God to trump a situation.

_____

_____

_____

_____

_____

_____

_____

_____

_____

_____

_____

_____

_____

_____

$\mathcal{D}ay\ 24$

THE GREEN MONSTER

MY HUSBAND, STEVE, IS A very charismatic, intelligent, and influential individual. When he walks into a room, his very presence commands attention. He has the ability to sell an ice cube to an Inuit. "You are able to sell with such ease because God created you to sell Jesus," I always remind him. We are very active in our community. We attend hundreds of social gatherings, fundraisers, and service club events, such as Rotary and our local Chamber of Commerce. He receives countless invitations to speak, motivate, train, and encourage others all across the country. He is consistently working on his next big project. With endless phone calls, texts, and e-mails, he is constantly responding, coaching, and pouring out late into the evening. He helps men, women, business owners, women, students, women, employees, women, women, women. Did I mention women? As his wife, I sometimes found myself feeling less than, inadequate, jealous even. We have attended events together where women have had the audacity to manipulate all his time, talking, smiling, and laughing at everything that came out of his mouth. They love rubbing his arms, exclaiming, "Oh, Steve, I never saw it like that before. You are a genius!" And at times, I get the feeling that he enjoys it as well. I know some of you reading this know exactly what I am talking about. I grew possessive, judgmental, suspicious, clingy, and needy. I began to suffocate him. I would check his phone call history to see who he called and who called him. I checked text messages, e-mails and voice mails. I even logged into his account to check his physical location.

I wanted to know where he was, who he was with, who he was talking to, what time he got there, and what time he left. The list goes on and on. I was an ugly green monster full of jealously and control. He would complain and say, "I will not be controlled by you."

One day I was riding in my car and pleading my case to God. I had just left an event with Steve, and there was another woman who completely ignored my presence and was all over him. I thought, *I know what she wants! She's not fooling nobody! I got her number. She had better watch her back!* Then my thoughts turned toward Steve. *Look at him. He knows what she wants. He's acting like he doesn't know, but he is not fooling nobody either. See God, it's not him that I don't trust. It's her. I know what she is thinking. I can see right through her!*

Then I heard God speak softly to my heart. "No, Erin, you don't trust me. It is really me you don't trust." Those words hit me like a punch in the face. God continued to speak to me. "See, if you trusted me, it would not matter to you who was in his face, where he went, or to whom he was talking. It would not matter to you what her intentions were. If you really trusted me, you would know that I am always working behind the scenes. I am your protector. I am his protector. And if you are doing all you know how to do as his wife and being all I called you to be as a wife, then believe that I am going to protect your marriage, and I am going to protect him."

Tears rolled down my face. God was right. I was not trusting him. God went on to tell me how he designed me especially for Steve, and no one could replace me. If I kept my focus on God, he would show me how to minister to my husband in a way that no other person could, that no other woman could. I was looking for Steve to provide what only God can provide.

Now do not get this message confused. I am not saying that you should not trust your spouse, but it should not be to a point that we lose sight of God; ultimately, our trust belongs to him. Today, if you find yourself jealous, possessive, suspicious, or controlling in any area, I encourage you to pray, talk to GOD, and give that area over to him. Begin to trust him with your whole heart. I promise you will not be disappointed.

Daily Prayer

Lord, today I submit those areas where I have taken my focus off you and started focusing on people, situations, and things. God, I give those areas to you; I put all my trust in you. I declare today that I will keep my focus on you for you are my fortress and my shield. I do not have to be jealous, controlling, suspicious, or fearful. Because you are for me, who can dare be against me? I declare you are Lord and God over every area of my life. In Jesus's name, Amen.

Scripture Reference

Trust in the Lord with all your heart and lean not to your own understand but in all your ways acknowledge him and he will direct your path. (Proverbs 3:5-6 King James Version)

Self-Reflection

Write a prayer to keep jealously out of your heart.

_____

_____

_____

_____

_____

_____

_____

_____

_____

_____

_____

_____

_____

_____

$\mathcal{D}ay$ 25

SHRIMP AND SAUSAGE CAJUN SKILLET

A FEW WEEKS AGO, I tried a new recipe. I was searching for some new things to cook and came across a recipe for shrimp and sausage Cajun skillet. The video showed step-by-step instructions on how to prepare the meal. As I watched the video, I became excited about making the dish. *The kids are going to love this,* I thought. I watched the video over and over again to make sure I knew exactly how to prepare it. The recipe called for shrimp, sausage, asparagus, squash, zucchini, red peppers, olive oil, and Cajun seasoning. The prep time was twenty minutes, and the cook time was twenty minutes, which made the dish even more attractive. I headed to the store. Excitedly, I shopped for every ingredient on my list. I headed back to the house to prepare my masterpiece.

The recipe called for all the vegetables and sausages to be sliced and diced, which was the longest part of the process. After the preparation, the recipe called for all the ingredients to be mixed in a large bowl, adding the olive oil and Cajun seasoning. I combined all the ingredients and mixed them together as instructed. The recipe called for the ingredients to be put into a skillet and cooked on medium heat until the shrimp were fully cooked. There was a warning on the recipe about the danger of serving raw seafood. If I didn't cook the shrimp until they were done, someone could get sick from eating this meal. As I was cooking and stirring the food, my mind went to the Lord. I remembered getting married when I was nineteen because I thought I was in love. I thought I was fully cooked and ready. The marriage lasted two years, and we both ended up hurt and damaged. "Why?" you may ask. Because we were not ready. We were still "raw" and "undone." To be completely honest, when I married my current husband, I was still raw and undone, but through God, we were able to grow and mature together.

I don't know what decisions you have to make today, but I believe God is saying, "Wait, don't rush. Stand still, and listen for a moment." Listen. God does not want us to enter into anything prematurely. He wants us mature and ready, so we will be able to stand. If you feel anxious, that is not God. If you feel rushed, that is not God. If you feel nervous, that is not God. Now, I am not talking about when you have heard clearly from God on a matter and you are procrastinating. That is different. This could be a relationship, a job, an opportunity, a business deal, a partnership, something where in the pit of your gut, you know it is just not right, or you have not received confirmation yet. Wait, be still, and God will confirm which way to go.

Daily Prayer

Father, today I pray for my brother and sister. I pray that just as your Word says, the steps of a righteous man are ordered by God. I thank you that you are ordering their steps. I thank you that you are lining up God-ordained relationships and connections. God, everything that is not of you, remove it now from their paths, close doors that no man can open, and open doors no man can shut. God, we thank you for divine intervention. In the mighty name of Jesus, Amen.

Scripture Reference

But those who trust in the Lord will find new strength. They will soar high on wings like eagles. They will run and not grow weary. They will walk and not faint. (Isaiah 40:31 New Living Translation)

Self-Reflection

Share an area where you are waiting to move forward and God is saying wait.

_____

_____

_____

_____

_____

_____

_____

_____

_____

_____

_____

_____

_____

Day 26

THE OPPORTUNIST

FOR THE PAST THREE YEARS, my husband has been traveling 70 percent to 80 percent of the year. During really busy months, he is practically gone every week, three to four days at a time. Being a business owner myself, and a mother of four school-aged children, the weight of him traveling began to take its toll on me. Each week, there I was, juggling kids, work, school, homework, dinner, breakfast, lunch, groceries, gas. I began to resent my husband. Especially on the nights he would text me pictures of himself in a fancy restaurant eating steak and lobster! The text inevitably would come in about the same time I was aggravated with one of the kids, or I was piecing a meal together after a long day. I thought, *What kind of mess is this? He is somewhere eating steak and lobster, and I'm here with these kids. He has the audacity to send me a picture of his gourmet meal! How selfish can he be?* I know none of you ever think wrong thoughts toward your loved ones; I know it is just me. But let me tell you, those thoughts had me feeling some kind of way toward my husband, and it wasn't positive.

During this time, the Lord was blessing us. Steve's business was growing, my business was growing, our household income was increasing. He was becoming known throughout the United States, and I was at home with an attitude. I had allowed "the opportunist" to start talking to me, and I listened. See, my friends, the enemy is an opportunist. He does not miss an opportunity to cause havoc in your life. He will not miss an opportunity to kill the hopes, dreams, and desires that God has put in your heart. He will not miss an opportunity to steal your joy or your peace of mind. He will not miss an opportunity to cause division or to destroy your relationships. But God! There is a but God in the scripture; there is a but God in the script.

I can remember the day but God showed up in my life. I was leaving the kids' school after dropping them off. It had been a rough morning, and nothing seemed to be flowing in the right direction. I began complaining to God about what I was feeling. I was feeling abandoned and left high and dry to go at it on my own. And God gently said to me, "Erin, I'm still here. Why are you mad at him? Don't you see the enemy's hand in this? He is the real enemy, not your husband. Your husband is doing what I called him to do. He is reaching people across this country. He is making a better life for you and the children. Why are you allowing the enemy to talk to you? You know he is an opportunist. If you give him a foothold, he will take it. You should not be surprised at the tactics of the enemy. If anything, by now you should recognize him for who he is, a liar."

Tears rolled down my cheeks because as God spoke to me, my heart softened. "He comes to kill, steal, and destroy, Erin. But I come that you may have life and have it more abundantly. I want you to have an abundant life. Trust the process. Trust me; I've got you. I've got Steve, and I am taking you somewhere." From that day, I have been careful not to listen to the opportunist when he talks to me. Oh, he didn't stop talking. I just stopped listening!

Daily Prayer

Today, God, I asked that you remind my brothers and sisters that you have come that they will have abundant lives. Remind them that the enemy is an opportunist, and he will take every inch they give him. He is a liar, and the truth is not in him. I declare that no weapon formed against them shall prosper, even the weapons we have formed with our own insecurities and disbeliefs. God, you are the author and finisher of our faith. We trust and believe in you, and you alone are God and Lord of our lives. In your Son Jesus's name, Amen.

Scripture Reference

The thief's purpose is to steal and kill and destroy. My purpose is to give them a rich and satisfying life. (John 10:10 New Living Translation)

Self-Reflection

Share a time when you know the enemy was whispering in your ear. How did God help you?

_____

_____

_____

_____

_____

_____

_____

_____

_____

_____

_____

_____

_____

_____

$\mathcal{D}ay$ 27

HUMPTY DUMPTY

ABOUT FIVE YEARS AGO, STEVE and I hit a rough patch in our marriage. During my career in the military, we lived in separate locations on several occasions. The stress of military life, raising children, working, and living apart, as well as the neglect of each other, had us on a fast path to divorce. Both of us had been unfaithful in our marriage, and the damage of those choices had begun to take its toll. Divorce seemed inevitable. We had grown apart and fallen out of love. Steve moved out and talks of divorce began.

As my marriage crumbled, the last thing I wanted to do was tell anyone. We had always been the couple people admired. Little did they know our marriage was in crisis. I was devastated. I knew we had problems in our marriage, but for so long I had told myself the lie that we were still okay. I was unwilling to change my selfish ways, and as a result, my marriage was falling apart. I finally opened up to my grandmother and told her what was going on. We call her "Ma-Dear." She is eighty-five years young, five feet nothing but a whole lot of Holy Ghost! She began to encourage me and to pray with me. She spoke life into me and into my situation. One morning when the kids and I were leaving for school, we went outside, and Ma-Dear was sitting in her car, parked in the yard. Surprised to see her there, I walked up to her and asked if everything was okay. She said she was there praying for us. She said God told her he was going to put this thing back together like Humpty Dumpty. "Humpty Dumpty?" I asked.

"Yes, Humpty Dumpty," she said with excitement in her voice and a huge smile. I was puzzled, but at the time, I did not have time to talk; I was rushing to get the kids to school. As I drove, I thought about what she said, and it continued to puzzle me. "Humpty Dumpty? What in the world?" I recited the nursery rhyme to myself and thought, *All of the king's horses and all of the king's men couldn't put Humpty together again.*

I pondered on that for the rest of the day. I called her that night and said, "Ma-Dear, what in the world does God mean Humpty Dumpty?" I began to quote the famous nursery rhyme, "Humpty Dumpty sat on a wall. Humpty Dumpty had a great fall. And all of the king's horses and all of the king's men, couldn't put Humpty together again."

"That's right! None of the king's horses and none of his men can put this thing back together. But God can!" She screamed. "God can put it back together, just like it never happened."

When she stated that, it rocked my soul. It brought life, hope, and faith back into me. I began to pray and seek God for my marriage like never before. I committed to the process of allowing God to heal me from the hurt, the unforgiveness, and the pain of rejection and neglect. I submitted to God so he could heal me. With the help of our pastor's spiritual counseling and six months of marital counseling, we were able to find our way back to each other. God completely restored our marriage, and it is now better than ever. We no longer fake it. It is real, and it is true.

I don't know if your marriage is on shaky ground or if you have challenges in your relationships at work, with a loved one, a father, mother, sister, or brother. But I want to tell you God is able to put it back together like Humpty Dumpty as if it never happened!

Daily Prayer

God, today I pray for my friend reading this. I pray, God, over any relationship in trouble and turmoil in his or her life. God, I ask that you restore, rejuvenate, revive, and rekindle the love and the passion in the relationship. Where trust has been broken, I ask that you rebuild that trust. Where there have been neglect and rejection, I ask you to refocus the couple's attentions and affections, first on you and then on each other. Where there has been infidelity, I ask that you give them eyes for only each other. Where there has been betrayal, I ask you to soften hearts so forgiveness may flow. God, we believe your Word that says you come for us to have life more abundantly. We thank you now for abundant relationships. In Jesus's name, Amen.

Scripture Reference

A thief is only there to steal and kill and destroy. I came so they can have real and eternal life, more and better life than they ever dreamed of. (John 10:10 The Message Bible)

Self-Reflection

What situation in your life do you need God to fix like it never happened?

_____

_____

_____

_____

_____

_____

_____

_____

_____

_____

_____

_____

_____

Day 28

NAME BRANDS

MY HUSBAND AND I DIFFER on things from what we like to wear to our favorite NFL teams. For instance, Steve loves Nike. He has too many pair of Nike tennis shoes with matching hats and shirts to count. I, on the other hand, love Adidas. I love their shoes, their sweat suits, their T-shirts, their hats, you name it. I am an Adidas girl. Now football, I love the Dallas Cowboys. Emmitt Smith is from my hometown of Pensacola, and ever since he went to play for them, I have been a fan. Steve, on the other hand, loves the Miami Dolphins. Although the Dolphins have not had a winning season since their perfect season in the seventies, he is a die-hard, true-to-the-team groupie! This NFL conflict has rubbed off on our children. Half of them root for the Cowboys and the other half root for the Dolphins.

To add insult to the Cowboy fans of the family, Steve has a Dolphins man cave. He has everything Dolphins in this room, right down to a refridgerator with the Dolphins logo plastered across it. Steve has Miami Dolphins socks, shoes, T-shirts, shorts, pants, toothbrushes, bottle openers, shoes, shot glasses, coffee cups, regular cups, and ball caps. (Don't get me started on the ball caps.) Even though the Cowboys are not properly represented in the man cave, I have a substantial collection of clothing, purses, and shoes that represent my favorite NFL team. When Steve goes out for leisure, he is either representing his favorite team or his favorite clothing brand. Me, same thing—I am either representing the Cowboys or Adidas. When I have on my

110

Cowboys gear, other Cowboys fans smile, cheer me on, and we have light conversation about whatever Jerry Jones has done in the media lately. We always depart the conversation with either, "We are looking good this year," or, "I can't wait for this season to be over."

As I watched Steve pick out a Dolphins hat from his collection of 150 to go with his outfit one day, my mind went to the Lord. I wondered how things would be in our lives if we represented Jesus every time we left our homes. If we were as intentional in putting on Jesus as we were in putting on our favorite brand or team names. "I want you to be as excited about putting me on as you are about putting on your Adidas or Cowboys garments," I felt God whisper to my heart.

I know God, I thought with a repentant heart. *I want that too. I want to be a true representation of you. I want people to notice your presence in me when I enter a room. I want people to want to learn more about you because of the life I live before them. I want to display your principles and your ways. I want your glory to be manifested in my life. I want to be just like Enoch. He walked with you until he walked no more.*

After I told God all I wanted to be for him, he simply said, "If you love me, you will keep my commandments."

"Yes, Lord, I do love you. I will keep your commandments. I want my life to put a smile on your face."

"Erin!" I was brought back to the present moment as Steve yelled my name. When I responded, "Huh?" he asked, "What do you think of this one?" proudly showing me the hat it took him ten minutes to select.

"It looks good, baby," I replied. But I was still thinking about my conversation with the Lord. I prayed silently, *God, let my life be worship to you. Let you be the name brand I represent more than any other name brand. In Jesus's name, I pray, Amen.*

Today, my friend, make a declaration, that no other name brand will be more represented in your life than the Lord Jesus Christ. Wear him proudly, boldly, and with honor for many are called to walk this Christian life, but only a few are successful at being a true representative of our Lord.

Daily Prayer

God, I want to wear you proudly. I want to be a true representation of your goodness, your grace, your mercy, your love, your forgiveness, your favor, your blessings, and your power on the earth. I declare today that I will keep praying, keep reading your Word, keep applying your Word to my life, and keep allowing you to form me and mold me. I know sooner rather than later I will be a reflection of you. In Jesus's name, I pray, Amen.

Scripture Reference

Now then, we are ambassadors for Christ, as though God were pleading through us: we implore you on Christ's behalf, be reconciled to God. (2 Corinthians 5:20 King James Version)

Self-Reflection

How can you better reflect Christ?

_____

_____

_____

_____

_____

_____

_____

_____

_____

_____

_____

_____

_____

_____

Day 29

THE ACADEMY

IN THE FALL OF 2017, we received a shocking call from our children's school administrator. "Mr. and Mrs. Wilmer, we regret to tell you that after the holiday break, you will have to find somewhere else for Judah to attend school. If we keep him here, on the path he is on, he will be unable to graduate." Judah was struggling in school, and it had become almost impossible to motivate him to do his schoolwork. He would be on track for about a month and then stop, on track, stop, on track, stop. It was a very frustrating pattern of behavior. We believe in discipline, but nothing was changing his behavior; prayer, punishment, encouragement, you name it, we tried it. This particular call was one, however, that we were not expecting. I was devastated and disappointed, not to mention downright embarrassed.

The previous year, I had looked into a military bootcamp for teenagers. Steve and I both have military backgrounds, and we agreed the military played an important role in our lives. This particular program, however, would require Judah to be away for six months. At that time, neither of us was comfortable with that. Fast-forward a year, and we were forced to make a decision that would impact our son for the rest of his life.

Our children attend a private Christian school. We are very intentional about their education and their learning environment. A Christian education was important to us, and we were willing to make the financial sacrifices necessary to afford it for our children. Judah did not see the value of our sacrifices. A public school was not an option for us. With Judah's repeated bad habits, mixed with the wrong environment, we feared he would end up in a worse situation. So the military high school came back up for discussion. I can tell you, as a mother, I didn't want to send my firstborn son away for six months. I barely allowed him to spend the night with friends. But something had to be done, and there was no way around it. I could not send him into the world unprepared and lazy with bad work habits. I knew the discipline and the skills I learned in the military were still with me. I prayed. I worried. I prayed. I worried. I was not feeling any peace in my heart.

I remember one night in particular. I could not sleep, I was so worried about sending Judah away. I was terrified about things happening to him. I played out every bad possibility in my mind. I was torturing myself. It was in the wee hours of the morning that I began to tell God all my concerns. "God, what will people think? This looks like we are not good parents. What if he gets hurt? What if something happens to him? What if someone messes with him? What if? What if? What if? What if?" I went on and on and on.

"There is nothing wrong with asking for help, Erin," God spoke softly to my heart. "I wish more of my people would ask for help when they need it. There would be far fewer suicides, mass shootings, divorces, addictions, and so forth. People have become too embarrassed to ask for help because they do not want other people to know they are hurting. They want them to think they have it all together. I will protect him. He is my son. I have a plan and purpose for Judah. He is my witness. He can be my representative there. Trust me." Those words were a lifeline for me. How I needed that confirmation from my Daddy God.

Those were the hardest months of my life. I wrote my son every day. I sent him scriptures and prayers. Our whole family wrote him every day. Not one day went by that he did not receive an e-mail or letter from us, telling him how much we loved him, missed him, and how proud we were of him. Our family grew closer because of that experience. Judah and his dad became closer. God used that situation to make himself real to my son. He will share his experience with you in the bonus chapter at the end of this book. Thanks to that military school, I know without a doubt Judah can handle anything life throws at him. He is more than a conqueror!

I debated about adding this chapter for so long, but I realized it is not about me. So many of us struggle with asking for help, whether it be with our children, our marriages, our careers, our health, or our mental states. We hesitate to ask for help, and most of the time, we never do. Today I want to expose one of the greatest tactics of the enemy. He wants to keep you isolated. He wants you to be too embarrassed, too ashamed to ask for help. He keeps us in the, "What will people think," prison. Today, release yourself from that jail cell and ask for help. Yell, "Help" from the rooftop, and get what you need to become a better version of you.

Daily Prayer

God, today I pray that we will no longer allow the enemy to isolate us by using embarrassment and shame. I pray that we will ask for the help we need in our marriages, relationships, careers, health and mental states, or wherever we need it. We will no longer allow ourselves to be isolated from our lifelines. In Jesus's name, Amen.

Scripture Reference

Let us then approach God's throne of grace with confidence, so that we may receive mercy and find grace to help us in our time of need. (Hebrews 4:16 New International Version)

Self-Reflection

What do you need help with?

_____

_____

_____

_____

_____

_____

_____

_____

_____

_____

_____

_____

_____

Day 30

RUNNING AROUND LIKE A CHICKEN WITH ITS HEAD CUT OFF

AS A MOTHER OF FOUR; the wife of an author, speaker, and coach; a business owner; an active church member; and an active community servant, my life can get pretty hectic. I have shared throughout this journal times when life has gotten overwhelming. There are days when I feel like I am in a never-ending whirlwind, being tossed back and forth, up and down and all around. My schedule as a financial adviser keeps me on the road most days, traveling back and forth between appointments. On weeks when my husband is out of town, a typical day starts with a thirty-minute drive to take the kids to school, a fifty-minute drive to my office, four to five appointments, another fifty-minute drive back to school to retrieve the kids, and thirty-minute drive home. Once home, the work continues, getting dinner prepared, homework completed, everyone fed, chores completed, baths taken, and everyone to bed by nine o'clock. This is followed by another thirty to forty-five minutes of threatening them to go to sleep, or I would give them something to help them go to sleep! Somewhere around ten, I collapse in my chair with a sigh of relief and wonder if I really accomplished anything that day. All this, to start again the next day with the same routine. Not to mention, every now and then, life throws in its infamous monkey wrench—a flat tire here, a broken dryer there, or a school project over there; you get the picture. I developed the habit of saying, "I am running around like a chicken with my head cut off!" That was my automatic response and literally how I felt. I didn't know if I was coming or going. I was busy but felt like I was not getting a single thing accomplished!

One day, my sister, Jill, was at my house. It had been one those days, and the weight of the day must have shown in my body language because she asked, "How are you? You look tired."

Before I even thought about it, I replied, "I am running around like a chicken with its head cut off."

She quickly responded, "No you are not!" I looked at her with a puzzled look, thinking, *How is she going to tell me how I am feeling! She doesn't know what kind of day I have had.* She went on, "You are not like a chicken with its head cut off. A chicken with its head cut off has no brain. It is rushing about behaving panicked and irrational. It cannot think because it has no brain. It cannot see because it has no eyes. It cannot hear because it has no ears. The body is dead; but it doesn't know it. You are not any of those things. Your steps are ordered and directed by God. You walk with purpose and intention. You have the mind of Christ. You are a child of God, so you do what he tells you. You say what he tells you. You hear him, and you obey him. You are nothing like a chicken with its head cut off. Stop speaking like that about yourself!"

I sat there stunned! Everything she said was correct. But I had uttered that expression so many times, I had come to believe I was just like that chicken. I imagined myself running around aimlessly, just doing things. I was convinced that was my life, so much so, I declared it at least once or twice a week. I shook my head in disbelief. How in the world did I fall for that one? I know the Word. I know the power of our words. I know that the power of life and death is in the tongue. I know I shall have what I say. I know every scripture about the tongue and about words. I felt God speak softly to my heart. "It is one thing to know these things, Erin, but it is a whole other thing to live it and walk it daily in your life. It is when the cares of the world come upon you that you fall back into old habits. That is the time to resist the temptation to revert but instead press forward toward a higher way of life, My way."

I thought about what He said to me and what Jill said. I began to play back my actions over the last couple of months. No wonder I had been feeling this way for so long. It was exactly what I had been declaring. Now, when I am asked how I am doing, I reply, "I am doing better." Because I am. I am becoming better each and every day. On those really trying days, I buckle myself in and I declare, "I will walk this day with purpose and intention because I know, although I may not see it at this very moment, my steps are ordered and directed by God. All things work together for the good of those called according to his purpose. I know I am called, so today, I walk with him."

Daily Prayer

Oh, God, I repent for speaking death and not life with my words. Help me to not dig my own grave with my words. Quicken me when the wrong thing comes out of my mouth. Help me to be disciplined in my thinking, so I will not become the wrong thing in my actions. I thank you that my steps are ordered by you. I thank you that you go before me, making crooked places straight. I thank you that you are the author of my faith. I thank you that you are with me every step of this journey, and you have never left my side, nor will you ever. In Jesus's name, Amen.

Scripture Reference

Death and life are in the power of the tongue, and those who love it and indulge it will eat its fruit and bear the consequences of their words. (Proverbs 18:21 Amplified Bible)

Self-Reflection

What are you saying about yourself?

_____

_____

_____

_____

_____

_____

_____

_____

_____

_____

_____

_____

_____

_____

Day 31

THE HOUSEPLANT

A FEW YEARS AGO, A plant given to me by a client had grown so well in my office, I decided to take a piece of it and take it home. I put the clipping in water so it could grow root. After the roots grew, I planted it. I placed the plant by the window at the front of the house. For several months, the plant bloomed beautifully. It grew and grew. Then I decided to take another clipping and repeat the process. The plant kept growing and blooming, and I kept taking small pieces and reproducing it again and again. I decided to take the latest piece, plant it, and put it in my bedroom.

I grew so many offspring that it was all over the front of house. I wanted to have some of it in the back of the house, so I purchased a really fancy flowerpot and stand. However, I noticed something different with this offspring; it was not blooming as well as the others. As a matter of fact, this one began to wither away. Because it was hidden in the back of the house, it did not receive the attention it needed to thrive. I neglected the plant so much it died. I was so disappointed that I just left the pot alone. The soil began to dry out until there was no evidence of life. Month after month, I would walk by the plant, look at it, and say to myself, "I've got to throw this pot of dirt out. I need to just go out and buy a new plant." For some reason, I would get busy, and another month would go by. The other day, I was in my bathroom, getting dressed, and I glanced at the plant. It had vines! Not just one vine but three healthy vines. "Wait! What? Oh, this plant is a fighter. I thought you were dead," I said to the plant. "But you were alive all along. Your roots must be deep and strong!"

My mind immediately went to God. I thought about how we have had promises and dreams given to us by our Father, and situations, life, and disappointments have appeared to kill those dreams. Our dreams appear dead! Our hopes looked dried up, just like the plant. Just then, I felt God say to my heart, "Remind my people of the dream I placed in their hearts. Remind them that just because it looks dead, the root of that dream is still buried deep inside them. Remind them that I have a covenant with them. They are my people, and I am their God. Remind them that I Am that I Am, and if I said it, will I not do it?"

So today, on our thirty-first day together, I want to encourage you one final time. This book was birthed in my heart years before it was ever published. I know, just like me, god has placed things in your heart, and you may believe they will never come to pass. There are divine appointments, divine relationships, and divine connections waiting for you. There are books, businesses, plays, movies, inventions, even world cures in you. Don't waste another minute. Step out on faith! When you move, God moves. It's just like that!

Daily Prayer

Father, today I pray that those dreams, projects, books, movie scripts, clothing designs, schools, hospitals, colleges, banks, and churches you have placed in my heart will come to pass. I know all things are in your perfect timing. However, God, I pray there be no more delay, procrastination, or hesitation on my part, that I move quickly in divine obedience to the sound of your voice. In Jesus's name, Amen.

Scripture Reference

I know what I'm doing. I have it all planned out - plans to take care of you, not abandon you, plans to give you the future you hope for. (Jeremiah 29:11 The Message Bible)

Self-Reflection

What dreams have God placed in your heart?

_____

_____

_____

_____

_____

_____

_____

_____

_____

_____

_____

_____

_____

_____

Bonus Day

AM I ALONE?

Written by Judah Wilmer

IT WAS EXACTLY A YEAR ago my parents sent me to a military academy because I was failing in school. The academy was designed to help teenagers get back on track through military training and structure. It was a bootcamp for teens. At the beginning of the program, I was as nervous as could be. I was in a new city, away from my family for the first time. And on top of all that, I was completely alone. The first night, I put my head down on my pillow and cried because I felt true loneliness. There was nobody there I knew, and I was scared. For a while, I felt dread and loneliness.

Then the first bully came along and made that place a living nightmare. I was bullied because the other kids saw me as privileged and treated me like I didn't belong there. It was horrible. It got so bad and so frequent that I was scared all the time. It happened whenever no person in authority was around. When I tried to ask for help, no one believed me. I got to the point where I was ready to quit. Fear set in because I didn't know when the bullying would happen. I became very angry.

Then the enemy started talking to me, saying, "If your parents really loved you, they wouldn't have sent you to this place. They knew you would get beat up. they were just trying to get rid of the lightweight." For a while I believed him. I stopped going to church; I stopped writing my parents. The only time I talked to them was on phone call nights. I had completely turned away from God. I doubted I even needed Him. This lasted a long time. I felt like the devil himself was at my front door, waiting for me to open the door and let him in.

Then all of the sudden, God came and saved my life. I was sitting on my bunk, polishing my boots, and my foot box was open. I dropped my polish, and it went in my foot box. It landed right on top of my Bible, which I had not opened in a while. I grabbed my Bible and opened to the first page my ribbon was set on. I'll never forget the verse I read, Proverbs 14:12 (New King James Version): "There is a way that seems right to a man, but its end is the way to death." I started to pray, and right then and there, I asked God to save me. I had been so close to death and didn't even realize it. I got through the program with no more incidents. I'm back home, giving glory to God.

Judah's Daily Prayer

Lord, I thank you for my life. Father God, I thank you for the many blessings you gave to me. Lord, I just want to say thank you. Thank you for saving me, Father. You saved my life, Father; you took me from the hands of the devil. You delivered me from him, Father God, and I just say thank you for saving me from him. Lord, help me to walk by faith. and not by sight when I'm in doubt, Lord, and not seeing the light at the end of the tunnel. Speak to me, Father, and help me see your light. Please, Father, never let me forget you. In the name of the Father, the Son, and the Holy Spirit, Amen.

Scripture References

For God so loved the world, that he gave his one and only Son, that whoever believes in him shall not perish but have eternal life. (John 3:16 New International Version)

The Lord is my shepherd; I shall not want. He maketh me to lie down in green pastures: he leadeth me beside the still waters. He restoreth my soul: he leadeth me in the paths of righteousness for his name's sake. Yea, though I walk through the valley of the shadow of death, I will fear no evil: for thou art with me; thy rod and thy staff they comfort me. Thou preparest a table before me in the presence of mine enemies: thou anointest my head with oil; my cup runneth over. Surely goodness and mercy shall follow me all the days of my life: and I will dwell in the house of the Lord forever. (Psalm 23 King James Version)

Self-Reflection

How is the Lord Jesus Christ your Savior?

_____

_____

_____

_____

_____

_____

_____

_____

_____

_____

_____

_____

_____

_____

Until We Meet Again

I HAVE SO ENJOYED THESE thirty-one days with you. I pray that you are better for it. I know I am. I pray your relationship with God has been strengthened by this book. I pray you pursue God like never before because of this book. I pray you find, follow, and pursue your God-given purpose because of this book. I pray you look for him in every day and in every situation. And, beloved, I know when you shut out all the noise of the day and look closely, you will see him. Be blessed and tell someone about *God's Chocolate Chips*. Remember, everything is sweeter with God in it!

Made in United States
Orlando, FL
17 November 2021